YOU MIGHT BE FROM MINNESOTA IF...

Kirk Anderson

MacIntyre Purcell Publishing Inc.

MacIntyre Purcell Publishing Inc.
194 Hospital Rd.
Lunenburg, Nova Scotia
B0J 2C0
(902) 640-3350

www.macintyrepurcell.com
info@macintyrepurcell.com

Printed and bound in Canada by Friesens

ISBN: 978-1-77276-130-6

Library and Archives Canada Cataloguing in Publication

Title: You might be from Minnesota if... / Kirk Anderson.
Names: Anderson, Kirk, 1965- author, illustrator.
Identifiers: Canadiana 20190101601 | ISBN 9781772761306 (softcover)
Subjects: LCSH: Minnesota—Social life and customs—Caricatures and cartoons. | LCSH: American wit
    and humor, Pictorial. | LCGFT: Cartoons (Humor)
Classification: LCC F606 .A53 2019 | DDC 977.6002/07—dc23

MacIntyre Purcell Publishing Inc. would like to acknowledge the financial support of the Government of Canada and the Nova Scotia Department of Tourism, Culture and Heritage.

FOREWORD

Growing up in northern Virginia (the state, not the Iron Range city – a key distinction for this book), there wasn't much I knew about Minnesota beyond the bumper stickers. "The Land of 10,000 Lakes," "Minnesota Nice," the entertaining accents – that all checks out.

But shortly after moving here, I learned something deeper about the character of this state through Minnesotans themselves.

One of the first things I did as a Minnesotan was to join a campaign to defeat an amendment to the state Constitution that would have denied marriage equality to Minnesota families. In the end, we did something extraordinary, orchestrating a come-from-behind win to help make love the law of the land well before the federal government followed suit.

It was a remarkable moment in Minnesota history, one defined by a spirit of inclusivity.

As a new Minnesotan, there were moments I felt embraced and alone all at once. Part of something bigger but still on an island. Transplants and immigrants know the feeling well. You strike up a conversation with a stranger only to get the warm response, "Oh, did you go to Hopkins High?"

Ours is a state full of contradictions.

In the coldest winters, our tourism industry is hotter than hell. We're modest to a fault but rank us lower than first on any list, and prepare to incur the wrath of a lot of very nice people. From running and biking in the summers to cross-country skiing and ice fishing through the winter, we're about as partial to the great outdoors as it gets. But year-round the *hygge* culture permeates the indoors with every shared shot of aquavit and every gathering around the fireplace.

Kirk Anderson brilliantly captures the contradictions that make Minnesota home.

You Might be from Minnesota If... is likely to elicit serious reflection from life-long Minnesotans, and will double as an onboarding guide for new Minnesotans and tourists.

— Minneapolis Mayor Jacob Frey

INTRODUCTION

The Peterson Field Guide defines a Minnesotan (*Frigidi taciturnus inresolutus*) as a domesticated primate with a fishing license and at least one boat. Minnesotans can easily be spotted in their natural habitat, Target, in their telltale parka-with-flip-flops. During the season when testosterone levels run particularly high, the male of the species exhibits flamboyant purple and gold plumage. Brawls ensue, but never to impress a mate.

Most anthropologists agree Minnesotans originated when Canadians first began breeding with Americans. They spend winters hibernating, in small dens on frozen lakes, or in larger dens in Florida. They live off their body fat and Netflix.

Due to a short growing season, Minnesotans long subsisted on wild rice and JELL-O salad, until they developed a highly evolved raffle system for acquiring meat. They began walking on two legs once they discovered they could eat food on a stick.

In recent years, many refugees have arrived in Minnesota, fleeing unstable and inhospitable regions, such as Wisconsin. These Wisconsin-Minnesotans have difficulty assimilating, chiefly because they pray to a different Sports God. Some say this is understandable, as the Minnesotan Sports God does not answer prayers.

Minnesotans have a written tradition and pass down their history in the form of runestones. Runestones are notoriously open to interpretation, and debates rage whether the Kensington-Alexandria area was "discovered" in the 1300s by Scandinavians, or by the bastard offspring of King Boreas and Princess Kay. Other theories include magic missionaries, space aliens, or the people who were already here.

Many thanks to fellow researchers Eric Anderson, Karen Anderson, Dave Brand, Nancy Brewster, Ron Brewster, Chris Briscoe, Ed Dickinson, Mark Fearing, Kevin Featherly, Kathy Henderson, Rob Hubbard, Tammy Nelson and Mike Sooy. Thanks also to Steve Sack, John MacIntyre, Vernon Oickle and Alex Hickey for tireless work in carbon dating the fossil evidence.

— Kirk Anderson, Mickey's Diner, St. Paul.
(I ordered the Sputnick Burger.)

YOU MIGHT BE FROM MINNESOTA IF....

Your fridge is divided into meat, cheese, fruit, vegetables, and live bait.

You've ever reassured someone that:

Which really isn't that reassuring.

You have entire government agencies
dedicated to mosquito control.

**When life gives you an icy hellscape...
you make ice palaces.**

You know why a gas station in Cloquet looks like it could have been designed by Frank Lloyd Wright.

You're culturally diverse.

You've walked across the Mississippi River.

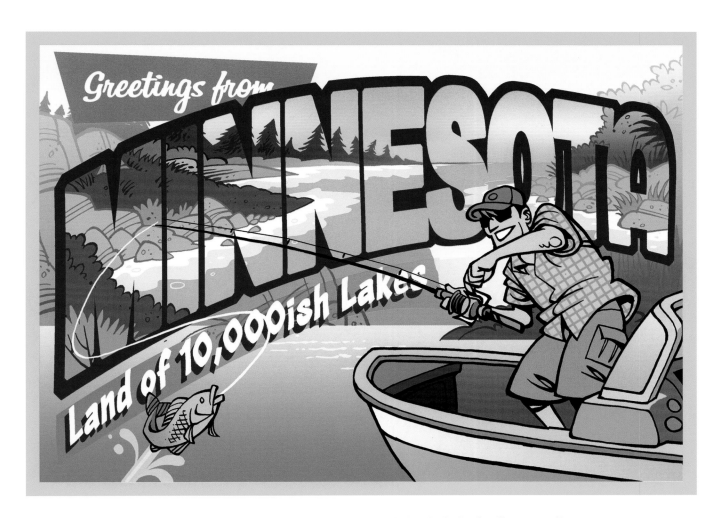

You just round it down to 10,000 lakes, because
11,842 would sound like you're bragging.

You politely refuse any offer of food
three times before accepting.

You *NEVER* eat the last piece of *ANYTHING, EVER.*

Your "wild rice" really is wild.

You're not afraid to try new things.

You welcome the totality of humankind.

... **individuals, not so much.**

Understatement is your unofficial state language.

Your idea of a pick-up line is:

You're not swayed by what 98% of the country thinks.

No, really; you're not swayed
by what 98% of the country thinks.

You brag about how much your weather sucks.

You *TRADEMARK* how much your weather sucks.

**You could teach Homeland Security
a thing or two about surveillance.**

You have the *WORLD'S BIGGEST HYPERBOLES!!!*

You fight for civil rights.

You remember civil wrongs.

You've heard a loon call in the wild.

**You know it's not a hotdish
until you add the secret ingredient.**

You think any food can be improved by infusing it with cheese, breading it, deep-frying it, wrapping it in bacon and putting it on a stick.

You know your state is one of the healthiest
in the nation, and you can't imagine why.

Your car has a winter survival kit.

In June.

You know why a Los Angeles team is named after lakes.

You appreciate Shakespearean tragedy.

Your amateur players beat Goliath.

You know how many inches of ice are required for a 2014 Ford Ranger vs. a 2016 Dodge Ram.

You can empathize with turtles.

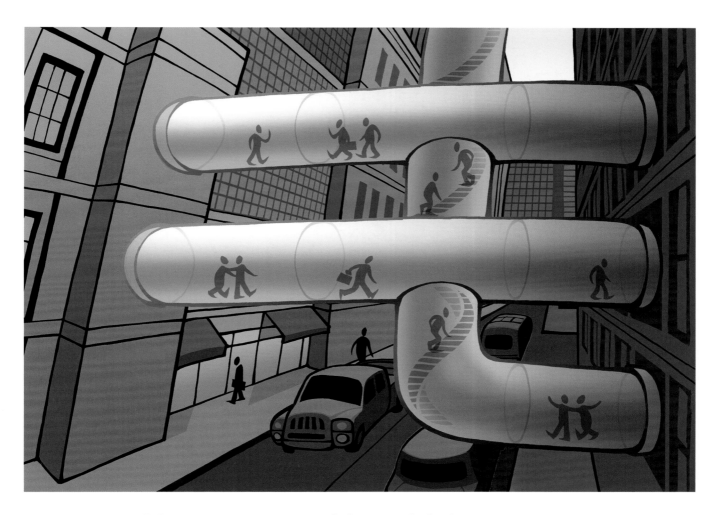

You can empathize with hamsters.

Your capital city's founder was an unsavory whiskey runner endearingly called "Pig's Eye."

George Bonga

You know the state wasn't established only by Northern European Lutherans.

You're innovative.

You're practical.

Even your *gambling* is practical.

Your neighborhood holds unscheduled team-building exercises.

**You heat your home the way God
and Paul Bunyan intended.**

You feed the bears.

You still call it Dayton's.

Your state name is a beer jingle.

You can follow directions.

... unless you're from St. Paul.

Like a modern-day Shackleton, you can't resist the stark, noble challenge of man against nature.

Your cultural ambassadors are immortalized in 90 pounds of butter.

You eat fish soaked in lye and flushed with water until it turns gelatinous and tasteless because, you know, *"tradition."*

You know what taconite is.

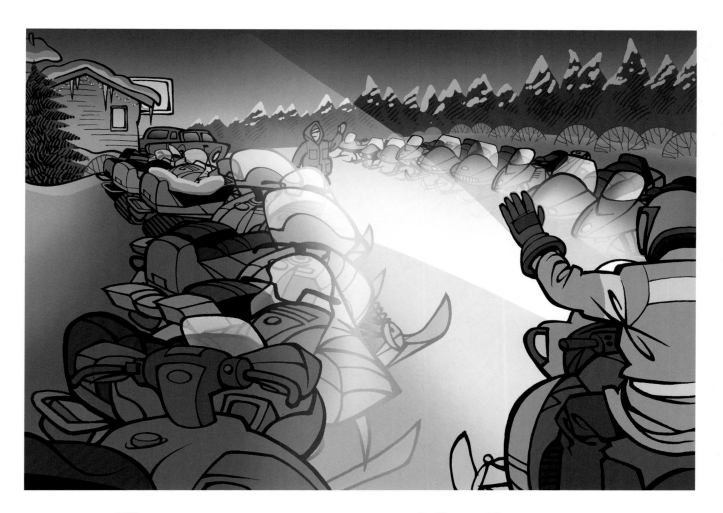

**There are more snowmobiles than cars
at your neighborhood bar.**

You know somebody who knows somebody who got invited to a 3am Paisley Park jam.

You're a survivor.

You've used your Target credit card as an improvised MacGyver ice scraper in a pinch.

You can make hockey out of *ANYTHING*.

Your small towns are so humble, they give themselves names like Embarrass, Motley, Downer and Nimrod.

**Kings and queens covet your state,
just to get a *colonoscopy*.**

You're unbearably polite, to the point of rudeness.

You're more diverse than you realize.

You were offended by that last cartoon.

You know the secret of the Kensington Runestone.

You know a sucker chub from a fathead minnow.

You could skate before you could walk.

You've been to a caucus.

You know what "DFL" stands for.

You believe in state-sponsored religion.

You're overregulated.

**Your employer gives 2 to 5%
of their earnings to charity.**

Once a year, your home town paves the street
with precious stones and free cash.

```
C I R C L E M E B E R T W O N Y W R S L O
F T D U O Y I J E L L O S A L A D K U Z H
O H P U B Y R R Y A N T H E L T C D R U F
R E R N L D A G R K E C I T E U R P E M O
T R I I B U N C A R T L P C S E B O D B R
S A N W T I T H O E B R I L K N Y S W R C
N N C N B A C H B M R N L S E S Y T I O U
E G E B O N S U Z E E I U M R D J I N T T
L E I Y O H O C V E T H D M A V R T G A E
L H A D T Y S I A S E L O L H O T D I S H
I M L R N L R P N L O L R M I I G W E C H
N D O A W D I E L Y W E P N E S P A M L P
G N L W E I E V P I E S K O L V I K E S O
O Y B R A R L M E B T O T X U T P G G P L
D J M W G L U D T B D R U W A T L O O E A
D G I M C R L O R N A O O D I B W A P N R
E F R B G A O E O I I I F C N N K M O D I
R O L Y W R W R Y S C F T L K R S P L Y S
N L O O N E C T S E U E T A C O N I T E T
```

You can find *at least* 15 Minnesota-related words.

(There are more than 40.)

You can tell which one doesn't belong.

You know which log cabin is on Lake Minnetonka.

STORY PROBLEM

It is 3:00, and the Finnegans are saying goodbye to the Schultzes. Julie Finnegan has soccer practice at 4:30. Practice is only a ten minute drive east, but she left her cleats back at home, 45 minutes due west. Kent Schultz needs to catch a 5:15 train, 25 minutes from the house. He has not yet packed. At 3:02, Pete Finnegan brings up Gopher football. Kent has strong reservations about the Gophers' defense this year, which he feels obligated to share.

It is now 3:20, and the Finnegans are saying goodbye to the Schultzes. Kent Schultz is mentally going over his packing list. Lorna Schultz asks Betty Finnegan how her tomato plants are doing. Betty has a funny story about an aphid infestation, which she feels obligated to share.

It is now 3:30, and the Finnegans are saying goodbye to the Schultzes. Julie Finnegan is mentally weighing the pros and cons of going to soccer practice without her cleats. Betty brings up the crazy weather they've been having. Everyone seems to have an opinion, which they feel obligated to share.

It is now 3:40, and the Finnegans have made it out of the Schultzes's house and into the driveway. They are not yet in their vehicle, although it is 12 ft. away. There is a momentary lull in the conversation. At what time will the Finnegan's vehicle actually pull away from the Schultzes's driveway?

You can solve this advanced calculus regional story problem.

You can find at least 20 things wrong with this BWCA scene.

(There are more than 40.)

85

You believe in the power of prayer.

Your homegrown chain outnumbers the Invasive Species.

Cabin fever occasionally affects your judgment.

You've bowled with a frozen turkey.

You suck at bragging.

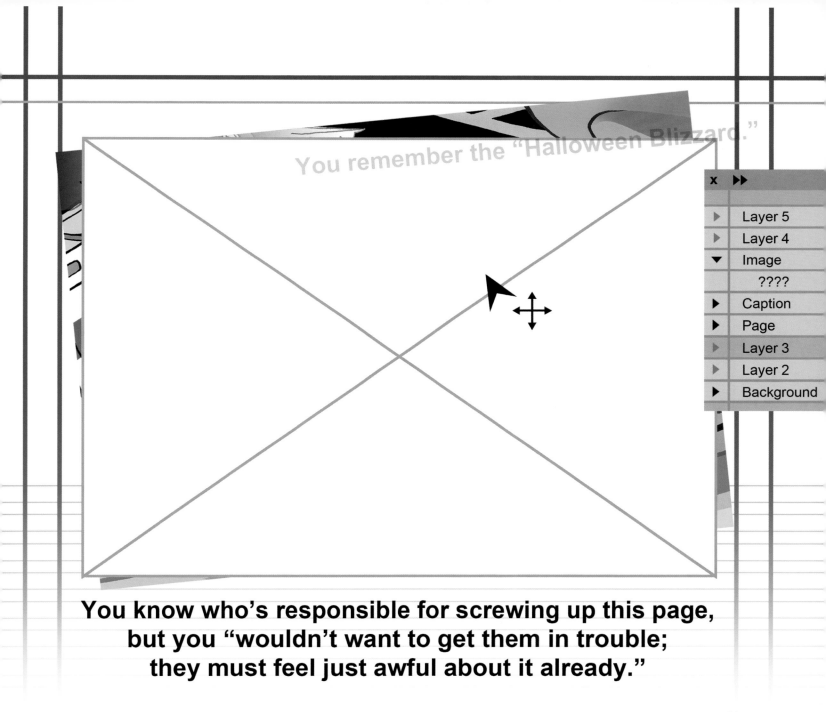

You remember the "Halloween Blizzard."

▶	Layer 5
▶	Layer 4
▼	Image
	????
▶	Caption
▶	Page
▶	Layer 3
▶	Layer 2
▶	Background

x ▶▶

You know who's responsible for screwing up this page,
but you "wouldn't want to get them in trouble;
they must feel just awful about it already."

You preface every meal with a full disclosure.

Your church's annual fundraiser is a 2-day 3-stage 20-band 120-decibel boozy outdoor bacchanal of rock. (And it's _Catholic_.)

You still haven't forgiven Dylan
for moving to New York.

You're towing at least one boat.

You spell your last name without prompting.

**Communicating negative emotions
is best left to the experts.**

These look familiar.

You've tried to pay your bar tab with beaver pelts.

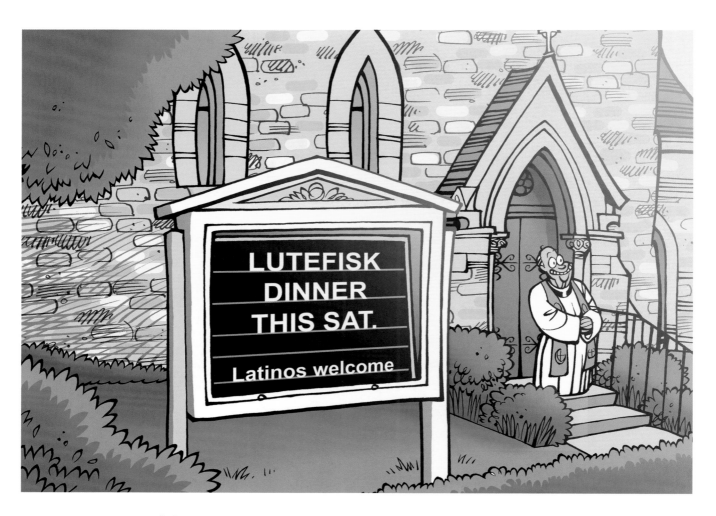

**You'd like to embrace diversity,
you just don't know how.**

You have snow tires on everything.

You've never heard anyone actually say "uff da."

You've been asked "The Question" so often, you've got your answer down to a 30-second elevator speech with bullet points.

You've seen 5,000-year-old graffiti.

You've seen a pantsless voyageur.
In public.

There's a snowplow on your wheelchair.

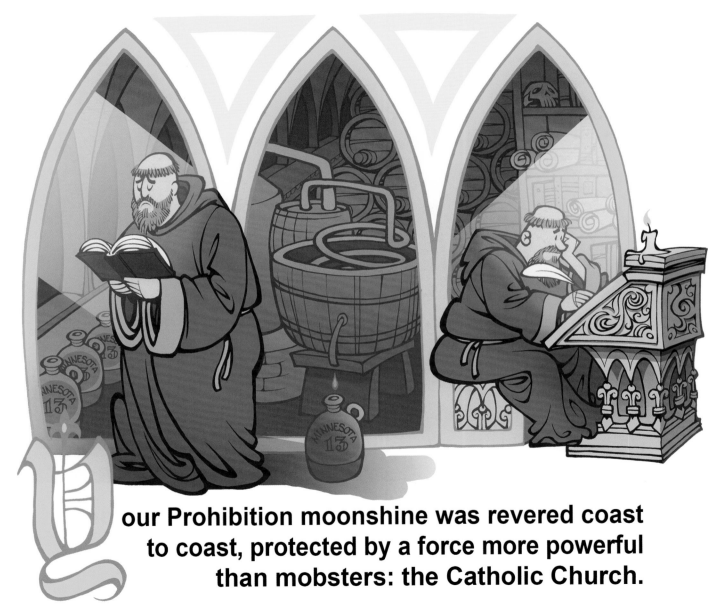

our Prohibition moonshine was revered coast
to coast, protected by a force more powerful
than mobsters: the Catholic Church.

Even your skyscrapers try not to look too proud.

You were taught that "the moral test of a government is how it treats those in the dawn of life, those in the twilight of life, and those in the shadows of life."

Your Crop Art scene is so advanced, it has its own school of Post-Impressionist Next-Big-Thingism.

Your government doesn't trust you with firecrackers.

When times are bad, you return to this sacred text
to show you The Way.

Your shrinking rural city is growing again.

You have never seen Fargo, out of principle.

You know everything happens for a reason,
and that reason is usually "building character."

You've taken a class at the North House
Folk School in Grand Marais.

Once winter hits, there's no looking back.

FOOTNOTES FOR OUTSIDERS

Page 10.   Yes, they really do use helicopters at the Metropolitan Mosquito Control District, although perhaps not in quite the manner depicted.

Page 11.   Ice palace from the 1888 St. Paul Winter Carnival. (It really was that ornate.)

The carnival began two years prior, to show east coast snobs we were not "another Siberia, unfit for human habitation," as one newspaper was sneering. The carnival was supposed to show prospective settlers — and critics — that sure, we may have 10 below zero weather here, but we can still frolic.

Page 12.   Indeed, it was.

Page 14.   The Mississippi River begins at the hallowed spot pictured, flowing out from Lake Itasca in Itasca State Park.

Page 15.   Wisconsin claims to have 15,000, but they count all lakes, which apparently includes puddles. In Minnesota, you don't get to call yourself a lake just because you're wet; you have to demonstrate to a panel of experts that you are at least 10 acres. Because in Minnesota, "Lake" is a title you earn, like "Sir," not some cheap honorific, like "dude."

Page 19.   Ilhan Omar, Keith Ellison, Mee Moua, Alan Page.

Page 20, 21.   The infamous "Minnesota Nice," welcoming and well-meaning on the outside, not so good on the follow-through.

Page 24.   In Reagan's 1984 landslide, Minnesota was the only state to vote for (native son) Walter Mondale. (DC did also.)

Page 25.   The only place on earth that doesn't say "GOOSE!"

Page 27.   International Falls literally trademarked "Icebox of the Nation" to stop Fraser, Colorado from claiming the honor.

Page 29.   Red Wing, World's Largest Boot; Eveleth, World's Largest Free-Standing Hockey Stick; Frazee, World's Largest Turkey; Madison, World's Largest Lutefisk; Darwin, World's Largest Twine Ball Rolled by One Man; Akeley, World's Largest Paul Bunyan.

Page 30.   The American Indian Movement (AIM) started in Minneapolis in 1968.

Page 31.   The notorious 1862 mass hanging of 38 Dakota men after the U.S.-Dakota War.

Page 34.   The immortal Minnesota State Fair, "The Great Minnesota Get-Together", is the second-largest state fair in the U.S. (Only second-largest?)

Texas' state fair attendance is slightly higher, but only because it's two weeks longer! In terms of daily attendance, Minnesota is number one.

Page 35.   Minnesota is usually in the top ten of healthiest states, sometimes numero uno. (How is that possible?!) We apparently have low rates of uninsured, heart attack deaths, and child poverty. However, we have high rates of alcohol consumption, and we apparently suck at vaccinations.

Page 36.   The NBA's first dynasty was the Minnesota Lakers, and the league's first superstar was Laker's center George Mikan.

Page 39.   The Minnesota Vikings' curse: some freaky act of God always intervenes to crush any Vikings playoff chances, including four failed Super Bowl attempts.

Page 40.   In the stunning upset over the USSR in the 1980 Olympics, Team USA was Team Minnesota: of the 20 players, 12 were from Minnesota, as was coach Herb Brooks. And the manager, goalie coach, physician, trainer, and equipment manager as well. It was largely Golden Gophers vs. the best of the Soviet pros. Sports Illustrated named it the No. 1 sports moment of the 20th century.

Page 42.   Portaging in the Boundary Waters.

Page 43.   Skyways.

Page 44.   St. Paul was originally called "Pig's Eye", after its most well-known citizen, Pierre "Pig's Eye" Parrant. Everyone seemed to know the guy who supplied the booze.

Page 45.   George Bonga, 1802-1874 — fur trader, guide, translator, merchant, entrepreneur — forged indispensable relationships with French Canadian traders, English settlers, and the Ojibwe. Fluent in all three languages, fluent in all three cultures, and, most importantly, trusted by all three interests, he was the cultural bridge that made early interactions possible. He was a guide and a translator for Lewis Cass, Henry Rice, and many others, and an advocate for the Ojibwe.

Bonga is regarded as the first African American born in what would later become Minnesota; he had an African American father and an Ojibwe mother. He was also legendary for tracking a murder suspect for five days and six nights in the dead of winter, and bringing the man back alive, tied to a dogsled, for one of the first criminal trials in the territory.

Page 48.   The ubiquitous meat raffle.

Page 53.   The Dakota called their ancestral homeland Mni Sota Makoce, loosely translated as "land of sky-tinted waters." Hamm's is an iconic Minnesota brand, having spent its first hundred years (1865-1965) in St. Paul.

Page 55.   North St. Paul is east of St. Paul, West St. Paul is south of St. Paul, and South St. Paul is east of West St. Paul.

Page 58.   The Dairy Princess, Princess Kay of the Milky Way, is sculpted at every year's State Fair.

Page 59.   The infamous Lutheran lutefisk dinners. Incidentally, actual Norwegians — i.e. those actually living in Norway — scratch their heads at why we might continue this laborious, outdated practice of cooking with lye for a less-than-flavorful outcome. "You do know we have refrigeration now, right?!"

Page 60.   Taconite, a low-grade iron ore, was once considered a waste product, back when high-grade iron was plentiful. The Iron Range was instrumental in winning the Second World War, but the war drained it of its high-grade iron. The mines were tapped out. In the 1950s, a technique was developed to harness the taconite, processing the iron into pellets, and the mines remained open.

Page 63.   1. Native Americans. Background on left: Columbus, Custer, Andrew Jackson, Martin Van Buren. Background on right, Minnesotans: soldier Josias King, Gov. Alexander Ramsey, Gen. Alfred Sully, Gov. and Col. Henry Sibley.

Sibley had good relations with the Dakota as a trader, but during his military career, he hunted and hanged them. He led forces in the Dakota War of 1862, which Gov. Ramsey presided over. During a post-Dakota War victory lap/revenge tour in 1863, Gen. Sully led an indiscriminate massacre of a Dakota village, complete with the destruction of animals, food, and basic survival tools, which soldier King participated in. Today, King is (unfortunately) celebrated, standing atop a St. Paul war memorial, as the first Minnesotan to volunteer in the Civil War.

2. Hmong (Laos, Vietnam, Thailand). The Hmong came to Minnesota starting in the mid-'70s, fleeing war in their homeland. Many Hmong fought as a "secret army" for the CIA during the Vietnam War. Minnesota has the second-largest Hmong population in the U.S., after California, and St. Paul has the largest Hmong population of any U.S. city.

3. Somali (Somalia). In the background: Al-Shabaab. Somalis came to Minnesota starting in the '90s, fleeing violence following the collapse of their government. Minnesota has the largest Somali population of any state, and Minneapolis has the largest Somali population of any city.

4. Karen (Burma / Myanmar). The Karen people began coming to Minnesota in the early 2000s, fleeing murder, torture, rape, and the burning of their villages. St. Paul has the largest concentration of Karen in the U.S.

Page 67.   The Mayo Clinic in Rochester is one of the most highly regarded hospitals on the planet, which is why its patients literally include royalty from half a world away.

Page 69.   Minnesota is still more homogenous than most states (approximately 80% white), but is changing relatively rapidly (from about 95% white in 1990).

Page 71.   Kensington (kinda near Alexandria), 1898: A farmer finds a rune-covered rock which purportedly proves that Scandinavians have been to Minnesota a century before Columbus' arrival. Is the runestone genuine or fake? We've been arguing about it ever since. Along with the origin of the Juicy Lucy.

Page 75.   Democratic-Farmer-Labor Party (DFL): In the '30s, the Farmer-Labor Party merged with the Democrats. Everyone still calls the Minnesota Democratic Party "the DFL."

Page 76.   We love our taxpayer subsidized stadiums. The public paid about 58% of the bill for the seven arenas shown, shelling out the most for the Twins ($350 mil, 64% of the total cost) and the Vikings ($678 mil, 62%).

Page 77.   It took the Legislature's special "Church Lady Bill" in 2011 to keep the jack-booted health code police from going full-blown pit bull on church potlucks.

Page 78.   Nice, honest, well-behaved, neighborly Minnesotans like their corporations to be nice, honest, well-behaved and neighborly as well. In 1976, 23 nice, well-behaved companies formed the 5 Percent Club, pledging to give 5% of their pre-tax earnings to honest, neighborly causes, and guilting others into doing the same. Today the club is known as the Minnesota Keystone Program, and recognizes companies donating at least 2% of pre-tax earnings to charity. The number of nice member companies has ballooned to over 250.

Companies that refuse to be benevolent are treated to ruthless Minnesotan passive aggression.

Page 79.   Moose Lake's Agate Stampede, part of the annual Agate Days Festival. Two trucks dump agates, gravel and quarters into the street. People show up with buckets, a starting horn blasts, and chaos ensues.

Page 80.   BWCAW, Circle Me Bert, Coya Come Home, DFL, don'cha know, Duluth, Dylan, eelpout, Ely, Fort Snelling, Grumpy Old Men, Hibbing, hotdish, Hüsker Hü, IRRRB, Itasca, jello salad, live bait, loon, Mayo, miigwech, Norm Green Still Sucks, North Shore, oh for cute, Ojibwe, Polaris, Post-It, Prince, Red River, Red Wing, Rondo, Root Beer Lady, Sioux,

Skol Vikes, Spam, spendy, Split Rock, taconite, The Range, ticks, Twins, uff-da, walleye, wild rice, you betcha, and Zumbrota.

Page 109.   Minnesota's moonshine epicenter was Stearns County; its "brand" was Minnesota 13[1]. Perhaps Minnesota 13's greatest selling point was that it wouldn't blind or kill you.[2] Apparently, the country trusted the sweet, diligent,[3] church-going moonshiners of Minnesota to make an honest product they were proud to stand behind.[4] And the Catholic Church gave their parishioners spiritual permission to support their families in unusual ways in tough times,[5] preaching from the pulpit that makin' moonshine was "illegal, not immoral."[6, 7]

Page 110.   Minneapolis' IDS Center (1972), Wells Fargo Center (formerly Norwest Center, 1988), and Capella Tower (formerly US Bancorp Place, and before that, First Bank Place, 1992), are all about the same height.

When the Wells Fargo Center and Capella Tower were built, the owners could have easily added a few feet for almost no cost and proclaimed themselves "Tallest and Most Important Building in All the Land". But that would just feel kind of disrespectful, you know? Just wouldn't be very Minnesotan, would it? So, they built lower out of deference. (Who does that?!)

Eventually, Capella Tower (or whatever name it was going by at the time — for a while it was simply known by the catchy handle "225 South Sixth") had some ventilation duct engineering hassle that required another 14 inches, making it taller than the IDS Center. Woohoo! Tallest in All the Land! But the owners kept mum, not wanting to ruffle any feathers. People eventually noticed the IDS Center had been dethroned, and Minnesotan discomfort ensued.

---

1   Minnesota 13: The name comes from the corn seed used to grow the main ingredient. The University of Minnesota developed the corn seed, named "Minnesota 13" (it grew in 13 weeks), to thrive in Minnesota's shorter growing season.

2   Wouldn't blind or kill you: Moonshine was completely unregulated, obviously, and thousands died from it as a result. Many moonshiners used lead in their equipment, lye in their process (for quicker results), and cleaning products for their alcohol content. Industrial alcohol was intentionally poisoned — by law — so people wouldn't drink it. Moonshiners tried to neutralize the poison with glycerin so people could safely drink it again. These efforts were not always successful.

3   Diligent: Between the Germans of Stearns County and the monks of St. John's Abbey, there was plenty of brewing and distilling expertise and pride. Stearns County moonshiners didn't take shortcuts; their whiskey was twice distilled and properly aged.

4   Proud to stand behind: The farmer who named Minnesota 13 also signed his own name on his bottles.

5   Tough times: Grain farmers were experiencing a depression. The previous decade, their grain fed war-torn Europe, and fueled horse-drawn transportation. That world changed in the 1920s.

6   Illegal, not immoral: The Church taught that there was moral wiggle room when it came to providing for one's family, and didn't see making alcohol as sinful. They were concerned Prohibition would come after the Church's sacramental wine next. At least one priest bailed parishioners out of jail, and let them know when the Feds were in town. One of the monks made stills for cash-strapped parishioners. The Church of St. Benedict was built with moonshine money (according to their own website).

7   Most of the above is based on the fun, fascinating, and well-researched book *Minnesota 13: Stearns County's 'Wet' Wild Prohibition Days*, by Elaine Davis (2007).

The unpleasantness was resolved when Emporis, a company that catalogs building construction data (Can you imagine your child ever saying "When I grow up, I want to work for a company that catalogs building construction data"?), decided to measure the IDS Center's height by including its window washing storage shed on the roof. The IDS Center was tallest again; equilibrium was restored, and folks breathed sighs of relief all along the Minneapolis skyline.

The late newspaper columnist Nick Coleman described the skyline as quintessentially Minnesotan: "trying to stand tall without standing out."

Page 111.   Hubert Humphrey was the patron saint of Minnesota politics. His nickname was "The Happy Warrior" for his upbeat determination to make the world suck less; he practiced what he called "the politics of joy," a term that we may sadly regard today as a bizarre oxymoron. It is said that he had opponents, but not enemies, and that he was effective in working across the aisle.

Humphrey played a key role in uniting Minnesota factions into the Democratic-Farmer-Labor Party. He became mayor of Minneapolis when the city was known as the "anti-Semitism capital of the country," and his reforms, including the nation's first fair employment ordinance, led to a dramatic decline in overt bigotry to Jews, blacks, and other minorities. Humphrey's famous speech to the 1948 Democratic National Convention, declaring "It is time to get out of the shadow of states' rights and to walk forthrightly into the bright sunshine of human rights," pushed the party away from its historic support for Jim Crow segregation. Humphrey originated the Peace Corps concept, was an early proponent of Medicare and the Partial Nuclear Test Ban Treaty, and was instrumental in passing the Civil Rights Act of 1964. Few have equalled his legislative accomplishments.

On the downside, there's his vice presidency and his silence on the Vietnam War.

Page 112.   One of many highlights at the Minnesota State Fair.

There is no blue ribbon for "Crop Art"; there are too many entrants with too much talent demonstrating too many subgenres. There is a blue ribbon for "Crop Art: Age 14-17 Division, Post-Impressionism," another for "Crop Art: Political Satire, Foreign Policy-Syria," another for "Crop Art: Cats Pulling Toilet Paper Off the Tube, Goth Seniors Division," etc.

Page 113.   If you want to play with gunpowder, you'll have to buy a gun; firecrackers are still too dangerous to be legal in Minnesota. However, in 2002, the legislature relaxed its death grip on pyrotechnic amusement and legalized sparklers!

Be advised that this reckless experiment in sparkler mayhem is for adults only; anyone who would derive actual joy from a simple sprinkling of sparks will legally have to wait until they're 18.

Page 114.   A 1973 Time Magazine story, featuring an exuberant Gov. Wendell "Wendy" Anderson and his latest catch on the cover, told the world about the amazing "Good Life in Minnesota." Affirmed at last! No longer would the coastal elites kick sand in our faces and refer to us as "flyover country"!

Almost a half century later, the magazine is still referenced by Minnesotans in a "Remember when we used to be somebody?" kind of way, whenever the state seems to have lost direction, or is questioning how to regain its mojo.

Page 115.   Cities like Worthington, Willmar,
        and Faribault would be declining if not for the
        immigrants filling their meat processing jobs
        and contributing to their economic growth and
        stability. Their schools have over 50% minority
        enrollment, and Worthington, far more diverse
        than the Twin Cities, has a total population that is
        over 50% minority. Their race relations have not
        been without problems, but they could teach the
        Twin Cities some lessons about living and working
        with a diverse population.

        Other cities in Greater Minnesota experiencing
        an influx of immigrants and refugees include
        Albert Lea, Austin, Mankato, Marshall, Moorhead,
        St. Cloud, St. James, and Owatonna.

Page 118.   The North House Folk School in Grand
        Marais has been teaching traditional northern
        crafts and cultural history since 1995, with courses
        such as woodworking, boat building, shoemaking,
        blacksmithing, timber framing, and hundreds more.
        Handy skills for when the apocalypse arrives and
        knocks out the power grid.

Minnesota Nice

**means covering the naked truth
with a warm winter coat.**